What Can You See by the Sea?

Written by Lou Kuenzler

RISING ★ STARS

What can you see by the sea?
Take a look!

Can you see the seagull fly over
the cliffs?

Can you see the puffins that live
on the cliffs?

Puffins fly down to the sea to get fish.
Can you see the fish?

Can you see the seal down on the rocks?

This seal swims near the coast.
The coast is where the sea meets the land.

Can you see the dolphins that swim in the sea?

Dolphins swim under the water
to get fish. Can you see the fish?

Now we are by the sea!
We are in the rock pool.
Can you see a crab?

cliffs

beach

rocks

seaweed

What can you see by the sea?
Take a look!

Talk about the book

Ask your child these questions:

1 Which birds live on the cliffs?

2 What do dolphins catch under the water?

3 Where can you see seals?

4 Where can you find rock pools?

5 What other creatures live in the sea?

6 Which animals would you like to swim with in the sea?